Fashion FORWARD

Prepped and Punked

Bringing 1980s and 1990s Flair to Your Wardrobe

by Allison Crotzer Kimmel

Consultant:
Clare Sauro
Curator, The Drexel Historic Costume Collection
Antoinette Westphal College of Media Arts and Design
Drexel University
Philadelphia, Pennsylvania

CAPSTONE PRESS
a capstone imprint

Savvy Books are published by Capstone Press,
1710 Roe Crest Drive, North Mankato, Minnesota 56003
www.capstonepub.com

Dedication: For Eric who gave me the time to write, for Mom and Dad who first
encouraged me to write, and for Aidan and Anneliese who inspire me daily.

Library of Congress Cataloging-in-Publication Data
Kimmel, Allison Crotzer.
Prepped and punked : bringing 1980s and 1990s flair to your wardrobe / Allison
Crotzer Kimmel.
pages cm. — (Savvy. Fashion forward)
Summary: "Describes the fashion trends of the 1980s and 1990s, including step-by-step
instructions on how to get the looks today"— Provided by publisher.
Includes bibliographical references and index.
ISBN 978-1-4765-4000-9 (library binding) — ISBN 978-1-4765-6161-5 (ebook pdf)
1. Clothing and dress—History—20th century—Juvenile literature. 2. Dress
accessories—Juvenile literature. 3. Fashion—History—20th century—Juvenile
literature. 4. Grooming for girls—Juvenile literature. I. Title.
TT507.K55 2014
646.3083—dc23
20130421196

Editorial Credits
Abby Colich, editor; Tracy Davies McCabe, designer; Marcie Spence, media researcher;
Jennifer Walker, production specialist

Photo Credits
Alamy Images: Jeff Morgan 11, 21, Moviestore Collection, 54 (left), Radius Images, 23,
redsnapper, 24, Trinity Mirror/Mirrorpix, 14, 30; Capstone Studio: Karon Dubke, 15, 17, 33,
37, 39; Corbis: CinemaPhoto, 32 (top), Herm Lewis/Kipa, 57, Mauro Carraro/Sygma, 44 (left),
Vittoriano Rastelli, 18 (left); Getty Images: ABC Photo Archives, 16 (bottom), Anwar Hussein,
7, Brian Smith/Bride Lane Library/Popperfoto, 12 (left), ChinaFotoPress, 42, China Pix, 32
(bottom), Dirck Halstead/Time & Life Pictures, 12 (right), Ebert Roberts/Redferns, 10 (left),
Emmanuel Dunand/AFP, 38 (top), Harry Langdon, 55, Hulton Archive, 22, Janette Beckman,
52, Jayne Fincher, 58, Jean Baptiste Lacroix, WireImage, 10 (right), Jim Smeal/WireImage,
51 (right), Devin Cummins/Premium Archive, 45, Kevin Mazur Archive/WireImage, 48, 50
(left), Mia Junior/BuzzFoto, 51 (left), Michel Ochs Archives, 34 (left), Michael Putland, 26, Ron
Galella, Ltd., 35, 38 (bottom), Stephen Stickler, 5, Terry Lott/Sony Music Archive, 28 (top), Tim
Graham, 8 (top), Time & Life Pictures, 40; iStockphoto: Arsela, 43 (blouse), izusek, cover (left);
Newscom: AFP/Getty Images, 20 (top), Bob Daemmrich Polaris Images, 20 (bottom), London
Entertainment/Splash News, 31 (right), smg/Finalpixx, 47 (left); Shutterstock: 360b, 41, Aleksei
Smolensky, 45 (boots), anyamuse, 53 (earrings), Artter, 45 (jeans), Creatista, 4, crystalfoto, cover
(bottom right), Elnur, 43 (shoes and purse), EM Arts, 11 (belt), Featureflash, 8 (bottom), 47 (right),
59, Gavran333, 19 (pearls), Hugo Felix, 36, il67, design element, irinap, design element, Jaguar
PS, 16 (top), 49 (right), Joe Seer, 18 (right), 44 (right), 50 (right), 54 (right), 60 (left and middle),
Karkas, 19 (skirt), 43 (skirt), Korionov, 9, kotss, 25 (T-shirt), lasha, 53 (necklace), ludmilafoto,
11 (shirt), maxstockphoto, 25 (earrings), Mitrofanova, 19 (sweater), NataLT, 27 (bottom), nito,
25 (leg warmers), NuDesign.co, design element, OZaiachin, 45 (hat), Petr Malyshev, 11 (boots),
photoban.ch, 53 (jeans), pil76, 27 (top), Richard Peterson, 25 (shoes), Roman Samokhin, 54
(boots), Ruslan Kudrin, 11 (skirt), 45 (shirt), 49 (left), 53 (jacket), s_bukley, 13, 28 (bottom), 31
(left), 56, 60 (right), 61, schab, 19 (shoes), schankz, 25 (scrunchie), Serg Zastavkin, 29, spotlight,
34 (right)

Printed in the United States of America in Brainerd, Minnesota.
092013   007770BANGS14

Table of
Contents

'80S AND '90S FASHIONS LURKING IN YOUR CLOSET

If you are wearing leggings, a cropped top, or sneakers, you have the fashion of the 1980s and 1990s to thank. Many current clothing styles aren't new. They are trends recycled from years past. Almost everything in your closet has a history. Much of that history can be seen by watching movies such as *Pretty in Pink* or a TV show like *Friends*. Dig into the '80s and '90s, and you might find a style that you already wear. Or you might find a forgotten style you can bring back.

Fashion trends gave the '80s its preppy charm and the '90s its carefree grunge. But the looks of these decades can be found in department stores and fashion runways today. In copying the clothing, hair, makeup, and accessories of the '80s and '90s, you'll recapture looks that ranged from simple to over-the-top. Many of these clothing choices continue to inspire modern looks.

ALMOST EVERYTHING IN OUR CLOSET HAS A HISTORY

5

BIG, BOLD '80s STYLE

The 1980s were a time of major political and social change in the United States. The 1960s and 1970s had been a time of rebellion and protest. By the beginning of the 1980s, people were ready for more stability. Americans became more concerned about working hard and making money. They also needed a break from the realities of work and money. Many people found it in the form of princesses and pirates.

In September 1980, the world met a shy preschool teacher named Lady Diana Spencer. Shy Di, as she was called, was engaged to marry Prince Charles of Great Britain, who would someday be king.

The real-life prince and princess were all over magazine covers in the months leading up to their July 1981 wedding. On that day 750 million people worldwide watched Diana become Princess of Wales. Her fairy-tale dress, designed by David and Elizabeth Emmanuel, became a sensation. Its train was 25 feet (7.6 meters), the longest on record for a British royal wedding. It featured large puffed sleeves and a silk taffeta skirt placed over a tulle petticoat.

Diana's wedding dress is the ultimate example of '80s fashion: large, dramatic, and romantic. But Diana became a style icon beyond her wedding dress. After her wedding, *Vogue* magazine's fashion editor Anna Harvey advised Diana on her clothing. They determined what the then future Queen of England should wear.

New *Princess*

Diana often took fashion risks. Today, Britain's newest princess, Duchess Catherine, continues to set fashion trends. Like Diana, Catherine caught the world's attention when she married Prince William, son of Charles and Diana. Some of Duchess Catherine's fashion trends include the use of nude colored heels and wearing modestly priced clothing from mainstream shops. When Catherine wears a dress, it sells out in stores soon afterward.

Get the Look

Diana famously wore an emerald and diamond choker that the queen had given her. Except Diana wore it on her forehead as a headband rather than around her neck. Create your own fairy-tale look by taking a traditional piece of jewelry and finding a new use for it.

SUPPLIES

- an old choker necklace
- bobby pins

1. Find a choker necklace in your jewelry box.
2. Measure it around your forehead for size.
3. Fasten it just below your hairline with bobby pins.
4. Now you have a ready-made headband fit for a fashionable princess.

Thar Be '80s Pirates Ahead, Matey

Part of the new romantic fashion of the 1980s included the pirate look, started by London designer Vivienne Westwood. Quirky 1980s performers such as Pat Benatar, Adam Ant, and Boy George used wild hair and makeup to set Westwood's high fashion couture to music. They wore lacey shirts under velvet jackets, tight black pants, and unruly hair. These fashionable followers of Westwood's '80s trend might just as easily been mistaken for Captain Hook. Modern-day pirates can take their cues from stars such as Johnny Depp, Russell Brand, and Helena Bonham Carter, who rock haphazard styles mixed with glam. Lots of disheveled layers, over-the-top accessories, and at least one long, skinny scarf complete the look.

Part of Vivienne Westwood's '80s style was a rejection of her earlier '70s punk designs. A few of these trends carried into the '80s, with torn clothes, T-shirts sporting rebellious slogans, and shredded denim remain popular. Pink, Gwen Stefani, and Avril Lavigne have let punk influence both their music and their fashion.

PAT BENATAR   GWEN STEFANI

PUT IT TOGETHER

Whether you choose to be a pirate or a punk, your style is sure to draw attention. To rock the full punk look, you will need these essential pieces.

Find a tank top in a bright neon color. Yellows, greens, and oranges look great.

Pair your top with a mismatched bottom. For instance, you may choose striped, leopard print, or even plaid pants or a skirt.

Your footwear should be military-style boots.

To complete that tough punk look, you will need a leather belt with spikes or studs.

Dressing for
Political Power

The world of '80s politics took a very different turn from punk and pirate fashion. Ronald Reagan, a former actor, was elected president in November 1980. His conservative policies helped to grow private businesses. Programs that helped the poor were cut back. His politics matched the change in attitude at the time.

Following his wife Nancy's example, people began buying flashier clothes from designer labels. The first lady hosted lavish balls for her Hollywood friends. Showing off your financial success with how you dressed was expected.

Americans became more image-conscious. They spent large amounts of money on the designer names and logos that became popular in the 1980s.

Even Margaret Thatcher, Britain's prime minister throughout the 1980s, brought her own style to the decade. Thatcher wore stiffly sprayed "helmet hair" and skirts with suit jackets. She proved that a woman could be feminine and in charge at the same time.

Women's suit styles have changed since the '80s. However, many women including Halle Berry still follow the "suit is power" model.

> A woman could be feminine and in charge at the same time.

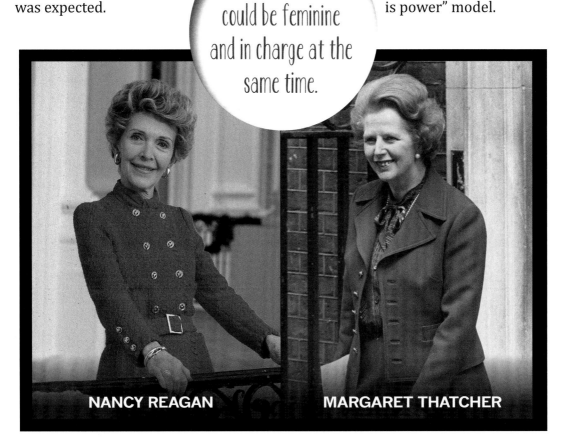

NANCY REAGAN **MARGARET THATCHER**

The Hollywood Reporter
Lifetime
L'ORÉAL
PARIS
WOMEN
ENTERTAINMENT

HALLE BERRY

Nancy Reagan and Margaret Thatcher modeled the trend of power dressing. Power dressing was a style of clothing that made its wearers look more skilled and confident. Influential women in the United States began dressing like these popular role models. This look included power suits and large, wide shoulder pads.

A popular 1988 film, *Working Girl,* showed the power of a woman in a suit. A secretary's idea is stolen by her boss. To steal her idea back, the secretary dresses in more powerful-looking attire.

Her new power suits and shoulder pads end up helping her career.

This shift in women's fashion was rooted in the fight for equal rights. For many decades, most women working outside the home in businesses were secretaries. The '80s brought women into leadership roles. To be taken seriously, women needed to dress powerfully. This often meant dressing like a man. Shoulder pads gave women a wider-shouldered silhouette. A female executive's suit jacket looked like one a man would wear.

Get the Look

Any shirt or dress can go from now to '80s shoulder pad wow by simply including two pieces of fabric and all the filling you can handle.

SUPPLIES

- large piece of fabric
- measuring tape
- scissors
- sewing materials

1. To get the size of fabric you will need to make your shoulder pad, measure your shirt from neckline to shoulder seam and subtract 1 inch (2.5 centimeters).
2. Make a circle with a diameter of that size, meaning if your seam measures 9 inches (22.5 cm), make an 8-inch (20-cm) circle.
3. Fold the circle of fabric in half, filling it with stuffing or batting.
4. Sew the open sides closed.
5. Tack one end of your shoulder pad near the shoulder seam and the second end near the neck seam.
6. Repeat these steps for the other side of your shirt.
7. Prepare to stun with your commanding shoulder pad presence.

'80s Fashion Goes Prime Time

In the early '80s prime-time royalty ruled the most dramatic looks. Nighttime TV soap operas such as *Dynasty* and *Dallas* featured powerful female characters. The costumes on these shows were very feminine in all their Hollywood glamour.

Many women of the '80s mirrored the dramatic appearances of *Dallas* and *Dynasty's* stars. Women's bold colored makeup, take-charge clothing, and big hair showed their confidence. Celebrities of today, including Heidi Klum, have followed this trend. They use bright makeup, elaborate hairstyles, and dramatic, over-the-top styles to show their self-assurance.

Get the Look

Big hair was all the rage in the 1980s. The bigger, the better. Characters Krystle and Alexis famously feuded on *Dynasty*, even pulling each other's hair. But none of that fighting could mess up their 'do. They followed two essential '80s rules for big hair—hair spray and teasing.

SUPPLIES

- comb
- hair pick
- strong-hold hair spray

1. To tease your hair, take a 2-inch (5-cm) wide strip of hair and lift it straight up.
2. With your other hand, comb the hair closest to your head backward toward the roots. Tease your hair slowly to avoid tangles.
3. Repeat this process over the crown of your head.
4. Lift sections of hair at the roots with a pick and spray heavily.
5. Spray the whole head to cover. If it holds up in front of a fan, you know you are soap opera ready.

Designer Fashion
Loves the Yuppies

> Yuppies loved making money and buying expensive things.

One of the most popular terms to come out of the 1980s was the word *yuppie*. Yuppie stands for Young Upwardly Mobile Professional. *Yuppie* is used to describe the 1980s ideal and the style that went along with it. Yuppies valued hard work and individual responsibility. They also loved making money and buying many expensive things, such as Rolex watches and designer bags. They wore leather, fur, and brand names on their clothing. Designers knew these professionals made enough money to afford their designs.

Yuppies loved to accessorize. Their earrings were famous for being huge. Many were large, plastic designs made with primary colors. They were also geometric shapes like circles, squares, and triangles with polka dots, stripes, or other patterns. For the 2013 Academy Awards, Halle Berry wore drop pendant black onyx and diamond circle earrings to go with her striped Versace gown. Huge geometric patterned earrings, especially featuring large dangles, are favored by Kelly Osbourne, Beyoncé, and the Kardashian sisters among others.

PUT IT TOGETHER

To get that Yuppie "causal cool," look for the three Ps—pastels, pearls, and pairs.

Find clothes in light pastels, like blues, purples, and especially pinks or peaches. White and khaki will also work well paired with '80s pastel.

Grab a long strand of pearls.

Pair your pastel Yuppie cardigan sweater with its perfectly matched pastel shell underneath. Drape your cardigan over your shoulders, tying the arms loosely over the front just below your collarbone.

Pair your pastel sweater combo and pearls with a khaki or white skirt. Finish the look with plain flats. White, black, or '80s powder pink will do.

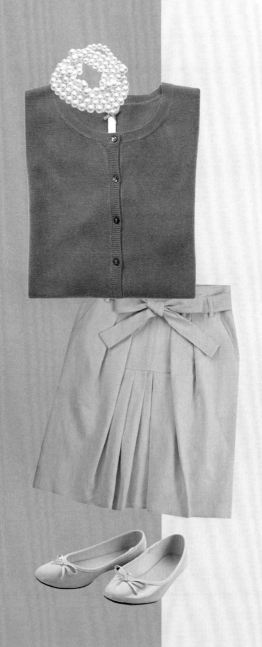

Designers Become Designer Names

In the 1980s many names in fashion design became recognizable outside the industry. One example is Ralph Lauren, who became known for his polo shirt. It is still worn dressed up with slacks or down with jeans. Lauren's polo shirts were recently used at the 2012 Summer Olympics in London. Team USA wore them as part of their uniforms. Supporters began wearing them too.

Calvin Klein, another American designer, invented the idea of the "total look." This meant you dressed in clothing that had the Calvin Klein label from your coat, to your shirt and pants, down to your underwear. A famous scene in 1985's *Back to the Future* shows the influence of Calvin Klein. Time traveler Marty McFly meets his mother when she was just in high school. She notices his underwear and begins calling him Calvin.

Calvin Klein

CALVIN KLEIN ADVERTISEMENT 1989

GOING '80S TO THE MAX

Fashion of the 1980s had its extremes. While there were the yuppies, there were also pop stars like Madonna wearing street styles. As many dressed up to impress, many also dressed down in sporty styles that came from the gym.

Get the *Look*

One major hair trend of the '80s was the side-pony. To go, like totally '80s, put that side-pony as high on your head as you can. It's radical.

SUPPLIES

- comb or brush
- ponytail holder

Pull your hair tightly to one side. Make sure there are no bumps as all your hair should look evenly smooth in the ponytail.

Preppies and Valley Girls

Preppy style came from casual sportswear attire associated with "prep" schools and prestigious colleges. But students kept this fashion long after graduation. They wanted to show everyone they would be successful in life, so they dressed the part. Required for every preppy's wardrobe was the Izod Lacoste alligator polo shirt. To imitate the '80s preppy look, push your collar straight up. Preppies also wore kilt skirts, cashmere, twin set cardigans, and tweed jackets.

In 1981 the hit movie *Chariots of Fire* was released. It helped make V-neck cricket sweaters a popular part of preppy attire.

A much-parodied look of the 1980s was the Valley Girl. These girls were from the San Fernando Valley near Los Angeles. They were typically wealthy and obsessed with clothing and shopping. Valley Girls put the California spin on being a yuppie. Valley Girls wore short, swinging skirts, stripes, leg warmers, and headbands.

PUT IT TOGETHER

Now you are totally stoked to tap into your inner Valley Girl. You will need five rad essential pieces to bring your look together head to toe.

All of your Valley Girl fashion pieces need to be pink, aqua, and striped.

First, find a headband to wrap around your forehead.

Find a pair of hoop earrings, the bigger the better.

Your shirt should be loose, neon, and patterned or plain. Bonus for choosing a shirt with a palm tree or California motif.

The only thing small about a Valley Girl's '80s style was her skirt. Choose a miniskirt in neon or denim.

The raddest Valley Girls wore leg warmers over heels with their miniskirts.

I Want
My MTU

Pop stars of the radio were brought to TV in 1980. Music Television (MTV) showcased music videos around the clock. It reintroduced some favorites from past generations, such as Michael Jackson. It also introduced new artists such as Madonna, who would go on to set various fashion trends across the '80s and '90s. Madonna seemed to reinvent herself with every new album release. Though she referred to herself as the Material Girl, her style of the streets attire shifted into high fashion in the 1980s. Madonna's iconic look featured lots of bangle bracelets, a messy tie in her hair, and leggings under a lace skirt.

Perhaps her best addition to fashion was the fingerless lace glove. These gloves differed from those associated with the poor and the tough. Because Madonna's fingerless gloves were made of lace, they were uniquely feminine. Girls of the '80s made their own as they watched Madonna's videos race across their TV screens.

Get the Look

Making fingerless gloves for the very first time? Here's how to copy Madonna's signature early '80s look.

SUPPLIES

- 2 pieces of lace each about twice the size of your palm
- scissors
- sewing supplies

1. Fold each piece of lace in half.
2. Place your hand on top of each folded piece.
3. Measure the pieces so that the folded edge of each piece sits at your knuckles. The bottom of each piece of lace ends at your palm. Cut off any excess material from the bottom edges.
4. Sew the side up. Then sew a hem, or border, around the bottom, leaving the glove open.
5. Cut a hole on the folded side for your thumb after laying your hand on top of the lace to mark where the thumb goes. You may leave the top of the glove open, or you may prefer to sew a small tuck, or closure, between each finger.

Michael Jackson became a star in the 1960s with his brothers in the Jackson 5. Now a young man, Jackson set out on his own. His 1983 album *Thriller* made him an icon in both music and fashion. One of Jackson's signature looks, the single white sparkly glove, debuted in 1983. He wore it during a TV performance of "Billie Jean." His other contribution to fashion was a red zippered jacket created by French designer Claude Montana. It appeared in the music video for the hit song "Beat It." The jacket became so popular there was a high demand for replicas. Red leather jackets have recently been seen on Alicia Keys, Ciara, and Fergie.

Pop sensation Cyndi Lauper also left her mark on '80s style. Neon and dramatic looks highlighted her style. Lauper wore vintage clothing in nontraditional ways. Always bright, her hair color frequently changed shades and was sometimes multicolored, partially shaved, and asymmetric.

Lauper wore her makeup dark and heavy. It featured dramatic splashes of eye shadow and lipstick in red or blue. Her accessories were piled on, with bracelets reaching up and down her arms and many strands of necklaces thrown together. Today's Selena Gomez, Kristen Stewart, and Drew Barrymore love to stack their bracelets.

Get the *Look*

Cyndi Lauper's mega-hit album, released in 1983, was titled *She's So Unusual*. Anyone sporting Lauper's signature eye makeup is sure to get the same reaction.

SUPPLIES

- bold-colored eye shadows
- eye shadow brush
- black eyeliner
- dark mascara

1. Choose an electric blue color and a secondary color that mismatches the blue, like orange or teal green.
2. Apply the electric blue eye shadow on the entire eyelid, from lashes to brow.
3. Apply that mismatched second color just below the brow line.
4. To further accent your eyes, choose black eyeliner with dark mascara, and "time after time," you'll look like Cyndi Lauper.

Stoked to Get Fit

Alongside the yuppie movement of the 1980s, a trend toward more casual dress was taking place. Like today's yoga wear turned casual fashion, popular sports and the fitness craze made their mark on '80s fashion. Wearing sneakers and workout attire outside the gym became acceptable.

Two major fashion trends to come out of the '80s fitness craze were leg warmers and leotards, especially in bright neon colors. The most popular exercise fad was aerobics, which included high-impact exercises with constant jumping, dancing, and muscle strengthening. Aerobics instructors led their classes while wearing headbands, tights, and legwarmers.

The tights aerobics instructors brought to '80s fashion grew into dressier looks in the form of leggings. And if you've worn a pair of leggings recently, you know these staples of '80s style were not left behind. But leggings of today do have some differences from their '80s ancestors. Leggings of the '80s had even wilder neon patterns. They were also worn with sweaters and oversized blazers.

Stars of today, like Sofia Vergara, right, wear their leggings dressed up with high heels. Others, including Eva Longoria, left, wear theirs more casually with boots for a fashion-forward look on the go.

Perhaps there is no better example of pop culture, fitness, and fashion merging than the 1983 movie *Flashdance.* Jennifer Beals' cutoff collar sweatshirt became the film's signature look. The cutoff collar allowed the sweatshirt to slouch and fall off her shoulders. The look became popular off screen.

Some of the *Flashdance* influence can be seen today. Celebrities such as Victoria Beckham, Katie Holmes, and Lauren Conrad pair skinny jeans with asymmetrical tops. These lop-sided tops hang loosely around the shoulders and taper to a snug fit at the hips.

Get the *Look*

Make your own *Flashdance* sweatshirt just as Jennifer Beals did.

SUPPLIES

- cotton sweatshirt
- scissors
- ruler
- pencil

1. Shrink the sweatshirt in the dryer so that its collar barely fits over your head. This will make the sweatshirt fit more flatteringly across your body.
2. Lay it flat for measuring and cutting.
3. Measure and mark with a pencil 1 inch (2.5 cm) above the cuffs of the sweatshirt.
4. Measure and mark two to three inches away from the collar of the sweatshirt. This will make the sweatshirt slouch to one side.
5. Cut the lines above the cuffs, and cut the collar out.

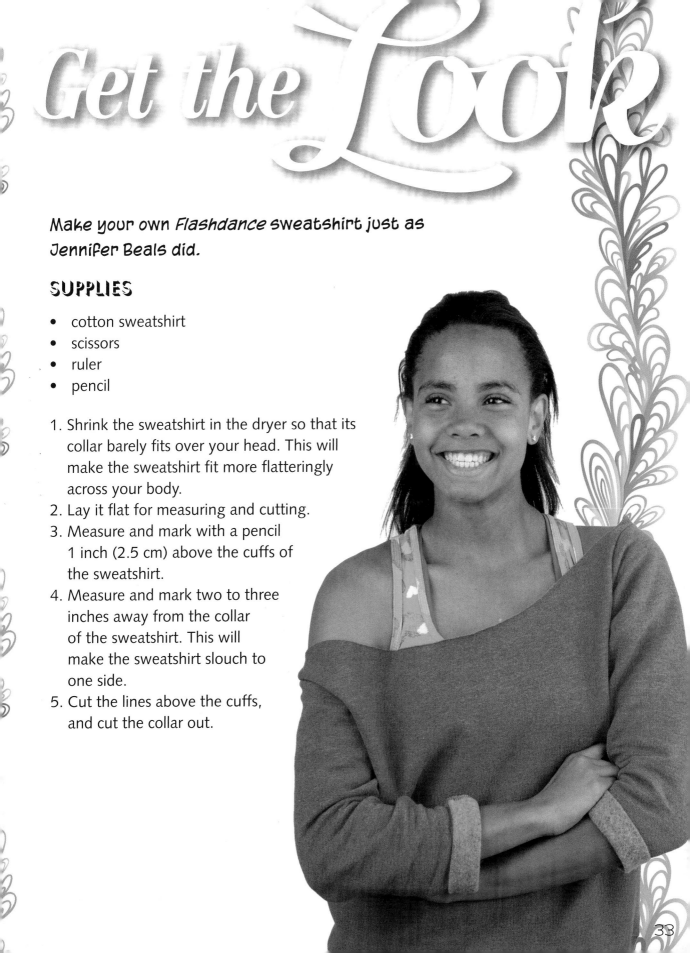

'80s Hairstyles

No discussion of '80s fashion is complete without mentioning a few more very large hairstyles. Many women found adding curl essential to their 'do. Perms, which meant treating hair with chemicals to produce curls, were a popular part of large hairdos. Teenagers, moms, guys in '80s hairbands, and professional men and women wore perms to give their hair lots of volume. The tighter the spiral, and the messier you could comb it out, the better. Jennifer Hudson recently sported a less messy perm.

Many men sported a signature '80s hairstyle called the mullet. Mullets were cut short at the front but kept long in the back. A popular phrase called it "business in the front, party in the back." The '80s female answer to the male mullet was the equally voluminous "wall of bangs." For women, the wall of bangs were teased and sprayed to perfection, often curled down, up, and sideways. Though current styles have yet to reach '80s heights, there has been a recent trend to cut bangs into long and short hairstyles. First Lady Michelle Obama, Taylor Swift, Kaley Cuoco, and Olivia Wilde sport bangs with longer cuts.

Get the Look

Reach new heights of hair excellence by creating your own wall of bangs. Remember the goal of large '80s bangs curl and spray them as high as they'd go. You'll want to use a lot of hair spray because once these things fall, look out!

SUPPLIES

- 1-inch (2.5 cm) curling iron
- strong-hold hair spray

1. Divide your bangs into two sections horizontally.
2. Take a 1-inch (2.5-cm) curling iron and curl the top half of the bangs straight up. It sometimes helps to add a touch of hair spray before curling to make sure the curl sticks.
3. Curl the bottom half straight under.
4. Take your fingers and separate the top half so that you get as much volume out of that top piece as possible. You can also curl the sides and feather them back with your fingers, making your bangs extend as far up, down, and to the sides as possible.
5. Spray, tease, and spray some more.

IT'S ALL GOOD: THE 1990S

If the key word of the 1980s was *excess,* the 1990s were more about simplicity. Another important word for the '90s was *change.* A new worldview, alternative styles of music, and a more casual sense of style spread throughout the decade.

Many changes took place throughout the world. With the birth of the Internet, communication across international borders was even easier. As the world shrank, fashion more easily moved from country to country.

Where fashion was once limited to certain regions, the opening of many major retailers abroad meant that clothing styles were shared.

In August 1990, Iraqi military forces invaded Kuwait, setting off Operation Desert Shield. A feeling of patriotic pride swept through the United States. People wore red, white, and blue. The American flag became popular on dresses, shirts, and jackets.

Get the Look

One '90s trend in accessories has politics to thank. The thick headband was most famously worn by then First Lady Hillary Rodham Clinton. Although the design has changed, the stiff headbands of yesterday are back in style today.

SUPPLIES

- 2-inch (5-cm) wide plastic headband
- hot glue gun
- scrap of fabric large enough to cover the headband

1. Line up your fabric, stretching it over the top of the headband with an extra half inch of fabric at both ends of the headband. The glued seam will be under the headband, so smooth out the top before gluing.
2. Start at one end of the headband and apply glue to that side.
3. Quickly press the edge of fabric over the glue and smooth it out down the length of the underside of the headband.
4. Pull the next side tightly so no bumps appear on top of your headband.
5. Apply glue down the second side.
6. Keeping the fabric tight, press it down over the second line of glue.
7. To finish up the ends, fold them inward under the headband and glue both sides.

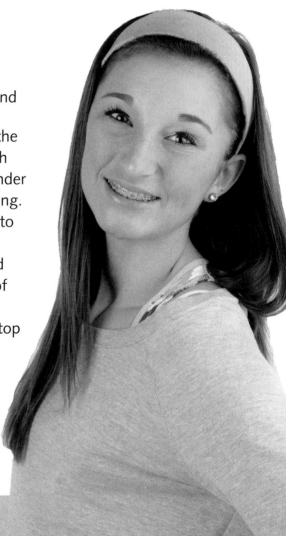

2013 USA GIRLS GYMNASTICS TEAM

PAULA ABDUL

The hair scrunchie, another accessory favored by everyone from Hillary Clinton to '90s pop star Paula Abdul, has recently reappeared. These accessories are elastic ponytail holders with gathered fabric that is made to stand out as it holds the ponytail in place.

Some of the Team USA girls gymnasts wore scrunchies on the gold medal podium at the London Olympics. During a 2012 fashion show, all the models wore them on the runway. Designer Marc Jacobs has even added colorfully printed scrunchies to his Marc by Marc Jacobs line.

Get the *Look*

Two things were certain at the beginning of the '90s. First, the United States loved red, white, and blue. Second, if you didn't have a scrunchie with you at all times, that might signal a fashion disaster. To show off your '90s savvy and your patriotism, make your own red, white, and blue scrunchie.

SUPPLIES

- patriotically colored fabric
- sewing materials
- 6-inch (15-cm) piece of elastic

1. Cut your fabric into a piece 4 inches (10 cm) wide and 20 inches (50 cm) long.
2. Fold the fabric in half lengthwise so that the printed side faces inward.
3. Sew only the side seem.
4. Turn the fabric pattern-side out and insert a 6-inch (15-cm) piece of elastic through the fabric tube. The elastic should stretch so that it touches and is sewn to each end of the fabric tube.
5. Put one end of the tube over the other end and stitch them together to make your stylin' '90s scrunchie.

SUPERMODELS
Are So Fly!

There were plenty of fashion models before the '90s. Some had gained personal fame, like Twiggy of the 1960s or Christie Brinkley of the 1980s. The '90s, however, brought a new idea of what a model could be. She was very tall, healthy, and athletic-looking. She also brought her own personality to the runway. This made her "super." These beauties with personality to spare easily became celebrities. The major supermodels of the '90s included Claudia Schiffer, Naomi Campbell, Cindy Crawford, and Linda Evangelista.

Evangelista was once criticized for saying supermodels didn't get out of bed for less than $10,000 a day. But she wasn't incorrect. In the early '90s these supermodels sold everything from soft drinks to cosmetics to hair care products. And they still found time to model beautiful clothing.

Many supermodels of today, such as Heidi Klum, Tyra Banks, and Gisele Bündchen, continue to be curvy, healthy, smart businesswomen. They not only influence fashion with their style, but also take on various business ventures.

GISELE BÜNDCHEN

COLOR
Blocking

A current clothing trend revived from the 1990s is color blocking. Color blocking means using solid colored clothing to emphasize the best body features. Colors are typically dramatically different. In the '90s it might have been black and white paired together. Models such as Cindy Crawford used the style to highlight their physiques. Now celebrities such as Kim Kardashian and Sandra Bullock have brought the color blocking style back to illustrate their chic sense of style. Today color blocking means pairing colors with their extreme opposites.

SANDRA
BULLOCK

PUT IT TOGETHER

You can easily build your own '90s color-blocking outfit. Start with two colors—one that is neutral and one that is bright. A neutral color would be black, gray, white, or beige. Examples of bright colors are green, blue, purple, orange, and pink. Make sure the clothing pieces you choose have no prints.

Many color blocked shirts of the '90s were silk, so choose a silky, flowing blouse or shirt. Pick a color like bright blue for your top.

Pair with a white skirt or neutral colored skirt.

To accessorize, choose a third color that is different from the bright color you chose in the first step. An orange purse and purple shoes will complement the bright blue top and white skirt.

Goodbye Yuppies, Hello Generation X

Fashion of the '80s showed the decade's riches. Fashion of the '90s, however, was affected by a recession and high unemployment. Clothing stores began offering major discounts to attract customers. Designers faced with financial cuts used cheaper fabrics, such as cotton. Young people of the '90s, called Generation X, were highly educated but underemployed. They preferred to buy clothing at bargain prices in thrift stores. Vintage clothing from the 1960s and 1970s, such as cardigan sweaters and worn, faded jeans, became popular. Kristen Stewart and Selena Gomez give worn, comfortable clothing a chic new twist.

PUT IT TOGETHER

To go grunge from top to bottom, start with a beanie hat in a dark color. It's important that you wear your beanie back on the crown of your head rather than pulled down over the forehead.

Wear heavily applied black eyeliner and bright red lipstick. Paint your nails black.

Choose a plaid flannel shirt with the buttons open the whole way down. Put it over a faded T-shirt.

Put on worn out jeans. The more rips and holes in your jeans, the more legitimately grunge you've gone. For that added grunge Gen X-er flair, take the flannel off and tie it loosely around your waist.

Finish your grunge girl look with combat boots or clunky Mary Janes.

Punk + Hippie = Grunge, "Oh well, whatever, nevermind"

In 1991 the band Nirvana released the single "Smells Like Teen Spirit." For teenagers across the United States, this song was their introduction to the grunge movement.

Grunge is a type of music that started in the Pacific Northwest. Beginning in the late '80s, artists such as Nirvana, Pearl Jam, and Soundgarden introduced grunge to mainstream America. The music mixed rock and roll with heavy metal and punk. Its musicians rejected typical '80s values of materialism and excess. Their look came directly from thrift stores and army surplus stores.

Grunge musicians dressed in ripped and faded jeans, long underwear under T-shirts, or old T-shirts under flannels. They also wore Doc Martens or old army boots, beanies over long, straggly hair, and cargo pants.

Typically described as lonely, lost, and bored, followers of the grunge movement rejected the go-getter ideology of the 1980s. Current celebrities such as Rihanna, Gwen Stefani, and Nicole Richie still favor the heavy boots and plaids that embodied the grunge style.

BABES IN TOYLAND 1992

Get the Look

Get easy, no-fuss, grungy hair.

1. Put your hair in a ponytail while it is still wet.
2. As it starts to dry, take the ponytail out. Leave the rubber band marks where they are.
3. Let the flyaways fly free.
4. Don't mess with your hair mess. Leave the brush on the counter so your hair looks as natural and unkempt as possible.

ASHLEY OLSEN

KRISTEN STEWART

ALL THAT AND A BAG OF CHIPS

Fashion designer Calvin Klein had predicted the '90s would be less showy than the '80s. His insight turned out to be quite true. Fashion became more about the look of everyday people. Trends shifted to a more casual look. This comfortable and informal dress contrasted the large shoulder pads and extreme designs of the '80s. Businesspeople began dressing in more casual attire at work. This led to an increase in khaki. The '90s also brought a greater use of denim.

BRITNEY SPEARS 1998

If You Stop by Gap,
I'll Come With ...

No retail store is a better example of this shift to casual than Gap. Gap opened in 1969 but grew more popular in the '90s. With its casual clothing and stylish image, the Gap look dominated '90s style.

In the '90s, however, many people preferred khaki to denim. Khaki pants, T-shirts, and neutral colors like grays, tans, whites, and blacks became staples in many closets. These neutral colors contrasted the '80s need for neon. Since the demand for comfortable fashion had increased after the 1980s, signature denim became popular. Bootcut jeans were the most popular cut to come out of the '90s. They featured a flared leg that was less dramatic than the bell bottoms of the '60s and '70s. These same casual signatures are still popular today. Logo shirts and sweatshirts, denim, and casual khakis are rolled out every season and are seen on celebs such as Kristen Bell, Hilary Swank, and Gwyneth Paltrow.

Babydolls
Aren't Just for Toddlers

Simple dresses were also a 1990s fad. The babydoll dress was particularly popular following the grunge movement. Celebrities such as grunge queen Courtney Love made the babydoll dress a popular, somewhat edgy fashion choice. Its empire waistline sits above where the waist naturally falls. The short hem gave it the appearance of a typical toy doll dress. Babydoll dresses could be worn on their own or paired with tights. Many '90s tights had lace around the ankle. Tights with and without lace have come back in style today. The babydoll dress itself remains popular with celebrities such as Carrie Underwood and Jennifer Hudson, and designers such as Stella McCartney.

Another popular dress of the '90s was the simple A-line style. This dress was narrower at the top, gradually falling into a wider bottom, like the letter A. The A-line dress looks flattering on every body type. It has been seen on modern actresses from Octavia Spencer to Sarah Hyland. The '90s made long skirts fashionable. Many of these skirts were covered with floral prints based on vintage patterns. The length of the skirt combined with the detailed pattern created a slimming effect. It hid any body type underneath it.

Underwear Becomes Outerwear

Madonna's look underwent another change at the beginning of the '90s. Her *Blonde Ambition* world tour featured her in designer Jean Paul Gaultier's conical bra and corset. This sparked the '90s "underwear as outerwear" craze. Most fashion followers weren't willing to pair a bra with pants and call it an outfit. But many wore sheer fabric shirts with lace camis, bodysuits, or bustiers underneath.

This "see through" look also inspired spiderweb sweaters, which are wide-woven with some type of tank or cami underneath. Now back in style, they are paired with less risqué lingerie underneath. Selena Gomez regularly wears her UNIF Ashbury crochet dress. Julianne Hough has been seen in a see-through Rag & Bone Exeter crewneck sweater made of lamb's wool.

Hip-Hop Fashion Is Da Bomb

Just as grunge influenced '90s style, hip-hop music entered the American mainstream and brought its fashions with it. There was a new interest in soul, funk, and rap. The look of its artists spread across cultures. Everywhere people began wearing baggy pants and extra-large shirts. Rapper MC Hammer popularized parachute pants. They were often paired with heavy black shoes. Both men and women loved bib overalls. The popular trend at the time had followers wearing either one or both straps down. Wearers included members of the R&B group TLC and hip-hop group Salt-n-Pepa.

Though hip-hop styles have changed, today's hip-hop fashion icons such as Nicki Manaj and M.I.A. still value statement jewelry and other accessories.

PUT IT TOGETHER

Here is your head-to-toe guide to '90s hip-hop style as spun by Salt-n-Pepa.

large door-knocker earrings, preferably gold colored, and choose even larger thick rope gold chain necklaces stacked over top of each other

color blocked silk bomber jackets

acid wash jeans

black or colored boots

Fashion of the '90s was heavily influenced by TV and film.

Fashion of the '90s was heavily influenced by TV and film. No film better portrayed the decade's fashions than 1995's *Clueless*. Alicia Silverstone plays a Beverly Hills student with an endless closet.

Clueless contributed many styles to '90s fashion, such as knee-high socks with platform Mary Jane shoes and plaid miniskirts. Perhaps *Clueless*'s most famous fashion contributions, however, were simple, short dresses. They had no pattern or decoration, thin straps, and were very tight.

The dress was well-tailored without lots of extra puffs and fabric. In November 2012 Rihanna wore a red reproduction of this dress to the GQ Men of the Year party.

Of many TV shows that influenced the decade's fashion, one was the sitcom *Blossom.* It brought a playful, vintage-inspired style to a preteen audience. Blossom's signature look was a hat with a large, fake flower on the front. This hat became quite popular, coining the term "Blossom hat."

Get the *Look*

To make your own Blossom hat, you will need just three supplies and to follow three easy steps.

SUPPLIES:

- a small velvet or colored straw hat
- a hot glue gun and glue sticks
- a large craft flower

1. Make sure the brim of your hat is folded back. If it is not, simply roll it up. You may need to reinforce this now bent brim with some hot glue.
2. Take the craft flower and glue it to the front at the center of the hat. The flower should be a vibrant color so that it stands out from the hat.
3. When the glue has set, wear your Blossom hat straight down on your head with bangs and hair peeking straight out.

MAYIM BIALIK
BLOSSOM

Cropped Tops
and the
Rachel

Beverly Hills, 90210 set several fashion trends. Babydoll dresses and cobweb sweaters were popular at the fictional West Beverly High. *90210* also popularized the half shirt, which was a cropped T-shirt showing the midriff. Celebrities such as Rhianna and Kendall Jenner have recently been spotted in half shirts.

Friends featured the three female characters who sported different looks that reflected their personalities. One already fashionable trend that was popularized by the show was the cropped sweater. It could either be short or long-sleeved and hit above the navel. Popular character Rachel Green often wore her cropped tops with cargo pants as singer Gwen Stefani does today. Some of the signature *Friends* looks included long skirts, bib overalls, and transparent shirts with strappy tops or camis underneath. *Friends* also popularized mock turtlenecks, sweaters and sweater vests, and knee-high boots with miniskirts. No greater trend came out of *Friends* than the infamous haircut dubbed "the Rachel." The mid-length choppy layered hairstyle was copied worldwide after Jennifer Aniston's character Rachel Green began wearing it in 1995. Fans the world over insisted on getting "the Rachel." People still take cues from celebrity hairstyles, whether it is Kerry Washington's faux bob or Michelle Williams' short pixie cut.

JENNIFER ANISTON

New
Statements
of the
'90s

By the mid-1990s the marriage of Prince Charles and Princess Diana was over. The royal divorce of 1996 ended Princess Diana's fairy tale, but it freed her style. She no longer needed to follow royal rules about what was appropriate. Her necklines became lower and her skirts shorter. She began wearing sleeveless shift dresses, which were simple dresses that hung straight from the shoulders with no defined waist.

Perhaps the most famous dress Diana wore in the '90s was a form-fitted black dress with a plunging neckline. Diana's daring new look reflected the global shift in women's fashion that was taking place. Women of the '90s were becoming more confident. As a result, they demanded that their clothing showcased their healthy female forms. Today celebrities such as Angelina Jolie aren't afraid to show a little, or a lot of leg, as she did in her black Versace at the 2012 Academy Awards.

PRINCESS DIANA

ANGELINA JOLIE

THE '80S AND '90S
ALIVE AND WELL TODAY

You have the '80s and '90s to thank for many of the fashion statements you are making now. Every generation of trendsetters borrows from the looks of previous decades. Today's fashionistas add their own spin to popular styles of yesterday.

The freedom and idealism of the '60s and '70s turned into the '80s era of conservatism and materialism. The '80s, or "Me Decade," was filled with material excesses that led to the '90s casual and less expensive styles.

The '80s and '90s can be found in your closet today. Sneakers for common footwear and workout gear as daily attire credit their popularity to the fitness crazed '80s. Fads such as leggings and babydoll dresses have re-entered today's closets. Though they may not be here to stay forever, they will probably come back into style again. Some trends come and go. But much of yesterday's clothing styles, such as comfort, professionalism, and individuality, are here to stay. They have become more than trends. They are style icons.

Embrace the styles of yesterday, but also tweak them to fit your own personal style today. No matter if it's classic or trendy, wear your fashion with confidence.

ALMOST EVERYTHING IN YOUR CLOSET HAS A HISTORY

61

Glossary

A-line (A-LINE)—having a triangular shape; A-line skirts are fitted around the waist and flare at the sides

cardigan (CARD-i-guhn)—a sweater with no collar that buttons in the front

crewneck (KREW-nek)—a shirt or sweater with a round neckline and no collar

crop (KROP)—to cut away part of something

hem (HEM)—a border of a cloth garment that is doubled back and stitched down

khaki (KAH-kee)—a fabric that is a light yellow brown color

neutral (NOO-truhl)—a color that does not stand out

nude (NOOD)—skin colored

pendant (PEN-duhnt)—something that hangs down

petticoat (peh-tee-KOT)—an underskirt often made with a ruffled, pleated, or lace edge

sheer (SHIHR)—very thin or transparent, such as fabric

vintage (VIN-tij)—from the past

Read More

Hunt, Jilly. *Popular Culture: 1980–1999.* A History of Popular Culture. Chicago: Heinemann Library, 2013.

Niven, Felicia Lowenstein. *Fabulous Fashions of the 1990s.* Fabulous Fashions of the Decades. Berkeley Heights, N.J.: Enslow Publishers, 2012.

Sonneborn, Liz. *Far Out Fashion: Bringing 1960s and 1970s Flare to Your Wardrobe.* Fashion Forward. North Mankato, Minn.: Capstone Press, 2014.

Internet Sites

FactHound offers a safe, fun way to find Internet sites related to this book. All of the sites on FactHound have been researched by our staff.

Here's all you do:

Visit *www.facthound.com*

Type in this code: 9781476540009

 Check out projects, games and lots more at
www.capstonekids.com

Index